Contemporary Catechetics Series

Prompted by many demands, a series of contributions to the "Writings on Catechetics" in the German publication, *Catechetical Papers*, now appear in book form. Selected for inclusion are those articles and essays of a particularly catechetical nature. The completed series of books will mirror the catechetical questions and problems of our day, as they are extracted from the "Writings" of the *Catechetical Papers*. Theoretical as well as practical themes will be chosen, in keeping with the aims and purposes of the magazine itself. This contemplated series will include essays on the development of new catechetical approaches, on the significance of Israel in religious instruction, and on the new insights into the teachings about "the last things," as well as on other pertinent catechetical issues.

FATHER JOSEF GOLDBRUNNER

Series Editor

CHRIST
AND THE
END OF THE WORLD

A Biblical Study in Eschatology

Franz Mussner

Translated by

MARIA VON EROES

UNIVERSITY OF NOTRE DAME PRESS : 1965

Imprimi Potest:

> Howard J. Kenna, C.S.C.,
> Provincial

Nihil obstat:

> Joseph Hoffman, C.S.C.,
> Censor deputatus

Imprimatur:

> Leo A. Pursley, D.D.,
> Bishop of Fort Wayne-South Bend
> February 28, 1965

Original German title:

WAS LEHRT JESUS ÜBER DAS ENDE DER WELT?

First published by Herder & Co. GmbH.,
Freiburg im Breisgau, 1958

CONTENTS

PREFACE

An Interpretation of St. Mark 13

The following interpretation of the thirteenth chapter of the gospel in St. Mark was first submitted in the course of three lectures which were given by the theological faculty of Trier for the city of Trier —which explains why the lectures were so formulated, so easily understandable for everyone. The same style was also used for their subsequent publication. The question concerning the teaching of Jesus on the subject of the end of the world arouses the interest of widespread circles among the faithful and, therefore, the response cannot be left unanswered. For that reason this publication is primarily pastoral, not scientific. It will be easy, however, for the expert to discern in these expositions the scientific effort which was involved in handling the difficult material on the eschatological teachings of the New Testament. This does not exclude the fact, we are well aware, that even scientific work, applied for the purpose of explaining scriptural texts, stands in need of a blessing by Him who is in truth the author of Holy Scripture. A short literary annotation has been added for those readers who wish to pursue the study of all questions treated in this book.

INTRODUCTION

The question concerning the "end of the world" has always been one of the most pressing ones posed by mankind, and this is especially true today. When the believing Christian raises the question about the end of the world, he does not go to soothsayers, astrologers or sectarians to receive an answer, but turns first of all to Holy Scripture. What is it that Holy Scripture has to say about the end of the world? What in particular does Jesus teach about it? If someone can, and *is* able to, give us authoritative instruction about this subject, it is primarily the Lord Himself. Natural science is also in a position to give us an answer, for example, by speaking about the "heat-death" of the world. The answers offered by natural science may be the correct ones from that point of view, and theology will be careful not to meddle, but nature is not the only part of our existence. Besides nature, there exists a second, equally important and perhaps superior, component of our existence and that is history—not in the sense of natural history, but as history consisting of human decisions, taken freely by man who is endowed with an intellect. The fate of man is certainly determined as well by his nature and his biological faculties, but man is determined to a much higher degree by the spiritual and moral decisions he makes during his lifetime. History progresses and receives its characteristic aspect, in contrast to nature, through the specific decisions formulated by man. This belongs to the actual facts of world history, and facts cannot be denied. For example, a certain human being may arise and be able to alter completely within a few years the political, social and economic structure of his time in perhaps half of the world. For instance: Alexander the Great, Napoleon, and the well-known tyrants of this century. According to natural science, however, the earth may be heading, in milliards of years, for its so-called heat-death because of a final equalization of energy; nevertheless each one of us knows that, based on historical evidence, this is not what will cause the "end," but that important occurrences not belonging primarily to the order of nature but rather to history will occur instead. The hydrogen bomb unloosens the forces of nature with terrific energy, but this is not an invention of nature, but rather one of the human mind! Man is not only flesh; he is also spirit. He is a person endowed with faculties to form free decisions in history; thus it is he who determines its course. And because man is also a spirit, his existence is not only a natural one but also a historical one. Consequently, the end of the world may not coincide automatically with the heat-death of the cosmos, but could occur quite independently, perhaps even tomorrow.

However, whether this event which we call the end of the world is going to take place tomorrow or the day after, or later on in several hundreds of years is something we will never really be able to know, because history rests upon the free decision of man and, let us not forget, even more on the inscrutable plan of God, and thus cannot be definitely foretold. Still, Jesus Christ, in whom we believe as our Lord and Master, has perhaps taught us many important things about the end of the world. In fact, they are of such importance that it is worthwhile to make the effort to find out exactly what He had to say on that point. What is it that Jesus teaches us about the end of the world? This is the question which calls for an answer, but this answer can only be given by keeping closely aligned to Holy Scripture. Its formulation will be an interpretation of the pertinent texts of the gospel.

In answering this question about the "end," Jesus went into details. Everything essential which He taught on this subject has been gathered and combined in the so-called synoptic apocalypse. The expression "apocalypse" is taken from the Greek word *apokalypsis* and means literally "disclosure," "revelation"; it is particularly used in the sense of revealing the mysteries of eschatology. The word "synoptic" is used in the professional language of exegetes to designate the first three gospels (those of Matthew, Mark, and Luke). The expression "synoptic apocalypse" must therefore be understood as the teaching of Jesus on the "end," the way it was handed down to us by the first three evangelists, the so-called synoptics. Historically it is not quite certain that Jesus gave His teaching on eschatology in one conclusive discourse. Rather, it is probable that the evangelists, or prior to them, the apostolic tradition, gathered everything that Jesus had to say about the theme, the end of the world, and combined it into the one discourse we now have in the gospels. We find this discourse on eschatology by Jesus in chapter 13 of the gospel by St. Mark (as well as chapter 24 of Matthew and chapter 21 of Luke).

At the same time we must also consider that Jesus was not the first and only one who taught about eschatological (apocalyptic) events. Much had already been said about these things by the prophets of the Old Testament, especially the prophet Daniel, and before him Isaias and Ezekiel. Furthermore, during the time of Jesus, books were written in Judaism, so-called apogryphs, which offered instructions about apocalyptic events; see for example, the books of Henoch. Those interested in obtaining further pertinent information may refer to the book by P. Riessler, mentioned in the literary annotation. Thus Jesus stood in the midst of a broad stream of apocalyptic tradition. Christ did not reject this tradition but, instead, overtook much of what He found, by weeding out and often purifying this literature from many fantastic exaggerations and Jewish nationalism. Consequently, many expressions and images contained in the apocalyptic teachings of Jesus and throughout the whole New Testament have their parallels in the Old Testament and the so-called Late Judaism. For a fuller comprehension of eschatological teachings of the New Testament, a thorough study of the preceding and contemporary apocalyptic, especially of the book of Daniel, is most important, as the New Testament presupposes the old one, builds upon it and brings it to fulfillment (see Matt. 5:17–18). The new aspect which the New Testament gives to apocalyptic instructions consists mainly in binding the eschatological events firmly and indissolubly to the person of Jesus Christ. He is the "Son of Man" who, according to the prophet Daniel, takes the kingdom of God up with Him and to whom judgment is given by God over the godless nations at the end of time.

In the following, to answer the question "What does Jesus teach on eschatology?" the thirteenth chapter of St. Mark's gospel will be constantly used and interpreted. At the same time, however, parallels and specific traditions taken from Matthew and Luke will be considered here and there when the necessity arises to clarify or complement the material found in the gospel of St. Mark. The text taken from Holy Scripture will be quoted first, and then the interpretation will follow.

The Apostles asked Jesus expressly about the "end," and so the evangelists then tell us what prompted this question directly; it was the prophecy made by Jesus about the destruction of the Temple of Jerusalem (Mark 13:1–2).

CHAPTER 1

Jesus Prophesies the Destruction of the Temple (Mark 13:1-2)

"And as he was going out of the temple, one of his disciples said to him: Master, behold what manner of stones, and what buildings *are here*. And Jesus answering, said to him: Seest thou all these great buildings? There shall not be left a stone upon a stone, that shall not be thrown down."

Jesus is in Jerusalem. For some time His enemies have decided to put Him away. They are only looking for the right occasion to seize Him unnoticed. Jerusalem has decided against Jesus the Messias, it has already rejected Him. "Jerusalem, Jerusalem . . . how often would I have gathered together thy children, as the hen doth gather her chickens under her wings, and thou wouldst not? Behold, your house shall be left to you, desolate" (namely, forsaken by God), that is, abandoned to its fate. According to the gospel of St. Matthew (23:37-38), this pronouncement of Jesus, so full of grief and resignation, was spoken directly before He left the Temple together with His disciples. Only a few days more and He will walk the bitter way to Golgotha. Now, as they pass through the Temple

district, through the great marble and gold en-
crusted halls onward to one of its wide gates, one of
the disciples is enthusiastic about all this splendor
and thinks that he should draw his Master's attention to the buildings as He walks along deep in
thought and full of sadness. "Rabbi, look, what
wonderful stones and buildings!" There was ample
reason for so much enthusiasm. When it says in our
text that "He was going out of the Temple," one
should not think of the actual Temple building as
such, which consisted of the holy of holies and the
sanctuary, but of the entire Temple district, with
its many buildings, halls and courts. Besides, King
Herod, with whom we are familiar as the murderer
of the infants in Bethlehem, according to the story
of Jesus' childhood, had decorated all these Temple
buildings in the Greek style. An old Jewish tradition
says: "He who has never seen the architecture of
the sanctuary (the building erected by Herod) has
never set his eyes on a building of real magnificence." Work on the building of the Temple was
continued after the death of the king and only finally finished in the year 64 A.D., shortly before
the outbreak of the Jewish war against Rome. At
this point, one should compare what the Jews once
said to Jesus: "Six and forty years was this temple
in building; and wilt thou raise it up in three days?"
(John 2:20). The Temple shone of gold and marble
and belonged to the seven wonders of the world in
antiquity. In gazing at it the simple man from Gali-
lee is overwhelmed by its splendor: "Look what
wonderful stones and buildings!" However, Jesus

remains surprisingly calm because He can foresee what is going to happen within a few decades to all this glory: "There will not be left even one stone upon the other!" Actually a few stones were left after the city was conquered in the year 70 by Titus, the Roman commander and future emperor, but not many of these stones can be seen today. Though the Temple had already been partly destroyed by fire when Jerusalem was conquered, "the Caesar ordered the whole city as well as the Temple to be completely demolished," as Flavius Josephus tells us literally in his history of the Jewish War. This is what Jesus is able to foresee, and therefore when one of His disciples points enthusiastically to the Temple's magnificence, His answer is, "The Temple will be destroyed!"

CHAPTER 2

The Disciples Ask About the "When" and the "Sign" of Eschatological Events (Mark 13:3-4)

"And as he sat on the mount of Olivet over against the temple, Peter and James and John and Andrew asked him apart: 'Tell us, when shall these things be? and what shall be the sign when all these things shall begin to be fulfilled?' "

       Jesus is sitting on Mount Olivet, "over against the temple," as St. Mark says. The mount of the Temple is situated on the east side of the town. From there it was possible to descend into the Kedron Valley by passing through a gate. One could then climb up the other side of the valley to Mount Olivet which was on the east side of the Temple, just opposite to it. As Mount Olivet was quite a bit higher than the mount of the Temple, one had—and still has—a wonderful view overlooking the whole Temple district. Jesus walks along with His disciples on the way leading from the Temple to Mount Olivet, and now He sits there, the Temple right in front of His eyes. The unexpected answer which Jesus gives to the enthusiastic exclamation of one of His disciples about the magnificence of the Temple must have preoccupied the Apostles' thoughts very much while they were walking along. And so those among them, who are very close to Jesus and in a leading position, Peter, James, John and Andrew, come up close to Him and ask the pressing question: "Tell us, when will this be and what will be the sign when all these things will come to pass?" The question is a dual one: first the "when" and then the "sign," that is, the omen.

This question addressed to Jesus is directly connected with His previous prophecy about the destruction of the Temple. But the way this question is formulated is typically "apocalyptic" and very similar in style to others found in the apocalyptic of Late Judaism and already in the book of Daniel. The question which the Apostles ask of Jesus encompasses in reality much more than the "when," the time of the Temple's destruction. It is rather a question about eschatological events, quite simply about the "end." The accuracy of this interpretation can be confirmed by the text of St. Matthew which runs parallel to this passage of St. Mark. ("Tell us, when shall these things be? And what shall be the sign of your coming and of the consummation of the world?") But why did the prophecy of Jesus concerning the destruction of the Temple induce the Apostles to ask Him about the "end"? This question was raised because the foregoing prophecy of Jesus caused their thoughts to turn involuntarily to the end of time. According to their viewpoint and that of their contemporaries, the destruction of the Temple belonged to the so-called Messianic pangs of birth which were to inaugurate the arrival of the kingdom of God. The prophecies of the Old Testament speak of a new temple to be built by the Messias, and this led to the conclusion that the old one would be demolished during this preceding period of "pangs." And thus, according to the Apostles' opinions, the Temple's destruction would initiate the last days of the world. That is why the prophecy of Jesus concerning the Temple's destruction prompted them to ask Him simply and directly about the "end," though Jesus had not even mentioned this in His foregoing prophecy. This is something which should be noted carefully: Jesus Himself had only spoken about the destruction of the Temple—and thereby He was thinking of the coming events of the year 70—but the thoughts of the Apostles, in posing that question, turn to the end of the world and not only to the destruction of the Temple. As we will see in the following, Jesus only answers the "apocalyptic" question of His disciples and discontinues to speak about the Temple, at least about its destruction.

In the first part of His subsequent discourse, Jesus warns His disciples not to take certain things as "signs" of the approaching end which, in reality, are not eschatological signs at all. And what Jesus has to say about this also is of the utmost importance for us Christians of the twentieth century.

CHAPTER 3

The Beginning of the "Pangs"
(Mark 13:5–8)

"And Jesus . . . said to them: Take heed that no man seduce you. For many will come in my name saying, I am Christ: and they will seduce many. And you shall hear of wars and rumors of wars. See that ye be not troubled. For these things must come to pass, but (compare Daniel 2:28) the end is not yet. For nation shall rise against nation, and kingdom against kingdom (compare Isaias 19:2); and there shall be pestilences and famines, and earthquakes in places: Now all these are (only) the beginnings of sorrows" (Matt. 24:4–9).*

The disciples of the Lord had asked Jesus bluntly about the end, the "when" and the "sign," and Jesus answers first with a warning—a warning against seducers: "Take heed lest any man seduce you!" Ernst Juenger tells us in his book *The Tower of the Saracenes,* in describing his stay on the isle of Sardinia in May 1954, that in the village where he lived there suddenly arose a rumor that on the following day, around midnight, the world would come to an end. Alarmed by this rumor, the people had flocked to the confessional in the village church, full

* St. Matthew's text is more adaptable to an English translation.

of fear, to await the expected event. We are all
familiar with this kind of report that circulates
from time to time, either based on astronomical
happenings, such as the appearance of a comet, or
because some types of sectarians merely spread
them around the world. Jesus warns us emphat-
ically against rumor mongers: "Take heed lest any
many seduce you!" The expression "seduce" belongs to the apocalyptic language of the New Testament. We run into it frequently in the Apocalypse of
St. John and also in the first letter of St. John. This
expression does not imply seduction in the moral
sense of the word, but rather in a sense pertaining
to matters of faith—a leading astray to heresy.

Who is it that the faithful are being warned
against? In verses 4 and 5, it says first of all,
do not let yourselves be seduced by those "who
come in my name." In Greek this could also mean
"under" my name, or sustained by my name. In the
course of time men will arise—Jesus even says
"many"— who will pretend in this world that they
are the Messias, the Christ, who has come back and
thus they will confuse and seduce the faithful, urg-
ing them to fall away from the true Christ. These
seducers will use God's own formula and say: "I
am He," namely, He Whom you were expecting all
this time; it is I who am at last bringing you salvation, the great joy and Paradise. This pretense will
cause many to be led astray and they will believe
in these false Christs and in their promises. Here
the text of St. Luke adds: "Do not follow after
them."

All these figures who in the course of history claim to be the true bearers of salvation, or the Christ who has returned, are not the only reason which might induce a follower of Christ, a faithful Christian, to believe that the end of the world is at hand. There are other things, which under the pretense of being "signs" for the coming end of the world, are being spread, like "wars and rumors of wars." The sectarians of our days delight in using these means of deception. They say that the end of the world is imminent because so many terrible wars have broken out in the world in recent years. However, Jesus says "fear not," as if this were already the end of the world, for wars must come again and again in the course of history as they are the result of sinfulness which disturbs the order of the world. These wars will be because "nation shall rise against nation and kingdom against kingdom." But they are "not yet the end" and certainly not "signs" for the approaching end of the world. Even other big catastrophes which will come upon the world and mankind in the course of time, namely, earthquakes, famines, and similar events, are not signs that the end of the world has come. All these phenomena of history which, according to the viewpoint of Late Judaism, signify the "pangs" from which the new world of God's kingdom will be born, are still not—terrible as they may be and much as they are always experienced as eschatological catastrophes in their respective centuries by their contemporaries (for example, the nights of bombing in the last war)—the true eschatological "pangs." They are rather "the beginnings of sorrows," as Jesus says. They certainly belong to the "pangs" which precede the future time of salvation but are not the ones that will directly initiate the end of the world. They are merely a beginning, pointing to that end which is sure to come some day—but nothing more.

It is important to call attention to all this because it might prevent us from falling easy prey to the rumors of these sectarians. Wars and other catastrophes of history and nature may seem very terrible and disastrous but, according to Jesus, they are not the signs for the sudden and near end. "Such things must need be," says Jesus with the words of the prophet Daniel; they are the necessary milestones in history, and nations will fall upon nations and one kingdom will supplant the other. These things will necessarily keep repeating themselves in the course of history, just as they have in the past, but they will not hasten the end of the world. That is why the invention of the atom bomb and the even more terrible hydrogen and cobalt bombs should not be regarded as eschatological events which will bring about the consummation of the world. However, there is, according to Jesus, one "sign" for the approaching end, but it is something completely different as we shall see. Even the hydrogen bomb belongs only to the "beginning" of "pangs," but not to the eschatological one which will initiate the end of the world. We should not allow the dreadfulness of these inventions to obscure a more serious view of things.

CHAPTER 4

Persecutions for the Sake of the Faith
(Mark 13:9–13)

"But look to yourselves. For they shall deliver you up to councils, and in the synagogues you shall be beaten, and you shall stand before governors and kings for my sake, for a testimony unto them. And unto all nations the gospel must first be preached. And when they shall lead you and deliver you up, be not thoughtful beforehand what you shall speak; but whatsoever shall be given you in that hour, that speak ye. For it is not you that speak, but the Holy Ghost. And the brother shall betray his brother unto death, and the father his son; and children shall rise up against the parents, and shall work their death. And you shall be hated by all men for my name's sake. But he that shall endure unto the end, he shall be saved."

With these verses Jesus shows us that before the actual "end" takes place there will be numerous persecutions of His followers; persecutions "in my name's sake," the way they have been and always will be everywhere and still happen in our present day. However, Jesus does not say that these persecutions are signs of the near end, else the world might have perished long ago. Instead, this paragraph closes with the sentence: "He who perseveres to the end (during the persecution), that is, to his death as that of a martyr, will be saved, namely, at the Last Judgment held by God." The persecutions of Christ's disciples thus belong inevitably to the interim period. At the end of this paragraph, in the gospel of St. Matthew, there is a sentence which says expressly: "But the end is not yet." Therefore the persecutions of the followers of Jesus are not in themselves "signs" of the approaching end in contrast to the viewpoint of Late Judaism, which saw in the persecutions of God's community a sign of the imminent end.

Now, just as the patience and steadfastness of Christ's followers during their persecution will be their salvation at the Last Judgment, held by the Son of Man over all, thus the work of those who persecute the Lord's community will be a "testimony against them." Jesus will say, "You have persecuted My community and now therefore you will be judged, but these others will be saved for life eternal."

Then Jesus goes on to describe in detail the persecutions of His followers. They will be delivered to the Sanhedrin and the Synagogues. These are the Jewish lawcourts, both small and large. They will be dragged before governors and kings and tortured. By this is meant the pagan law courts. When St. Mark wrote this text the Church had already experienced the truth of these words of Jesus. For quite some time the Apostles and Christians were already being delivered to the Jewish and pagan courts of law; here one should be reminded of the Jewish persecutions whose victims were Stephen and James the Greater (compare Apoc. 6:8; 8:4; 12:1–5), and of the great persecutions of the Church under the emperor Nero, whose victims were Peter and Paul. Parents will betray their children and children their parents to the authorities and thus deliver them to martyrdom. How often have we read in our own day that children betrayed their parents for being Christians in disguise and such acts were even encouraged by the authorities. This reminds us of something else Jesus said, "Think ye that I am come to give peace on earth? I tell you, no; but separation. For there shall be from henceforth five in one house divided: three against two, and two against three. The father *shall be divided* against the son, and the son against the father, the mother against the daughter, and the daughter against the mother, the mother in law against her daughter in law, and the daughter in law against her mother in law" (Luke 12:51–53; compare Matt. 10: 34–36). Jesus demands a decision of men which is even capable of separating and antagonizing whole families. Christian experiences confirm this definitely. "And you shall be hated by all men for my name's sake . . ." (Matt. 10:22). He who openly bears witness to Christ in time of persecution, brings down the universal hatred of the world upon himself. To avoid this hate by denying Christ is a big temptation for unfaithfulness during a period of persecution.

Apparently Jesus primarily spoke these words about the persecutions of His disciples in another context. In the gospel of St. Matthew they can be found as early as in the tenth chapter, but St. Mark inserted them here to refute the viewpoint that persecutions of the kind the Church had already experienced and will always experience were supposed to be signs of the approaching end of the world. Rather, these persecutions belong to the interim period—and this inevitably so, else the Church would not be the true community of Jesus.

At this point, in the middle of the Lord's teaching about the persecutions of His followers, St. Mark adds another pronouncement of Jesus, which St. Matthew places at the end of this paragraph: "And unto all nations the gospel must first be preached . . . ," namely, before the end is actually able to come. Thus, it is the will of God; this is implied by the mysterious-sounding "must." Now, this pronouncement of Jesus does not mean that the gospel actually has to be accepted by all nations, in the sense that the majority of all inhabitants of these nations will have to become Christians. Rather, it signifies that the gospel must be announced to all nations, that is, all nations must be faced with the possibility of deciding for or against Christ: to either follow obediently the message of redemption given to us by Jesus Christ or to refuse it. As to whether or not all nations have already come into contact with the gospel in our days can be answered in the affirmative, but to conclude therefrom that the end of the world is imminent is certainly wrong.

The pronouncement of Jesus concerning the spreading of the gospel among all nations is significant only in the context that the end cannot possibly come before the gospel is preached to all, but it does not mean that this is a sign of the near end and the coming of Christ.

CHAPTER 5

The Height of Tribulations During the Persecutions at the Time of the Antichrist (Mark 13:14–23)

"And when you shall see the abomination of deso-lation, standing where it ought not: he that readeth let him understand: then let them that are in Judea, flee unto the mountains: And let him that is on the housetop, not go down into the house, nor enter therein to take anything out of the house: And let him that shall be in the field, not turn back to take up his garment. And woe to them that are with child, and that give suck in those days. But pray ye, that these things happen not in winter. For in those days shall be such tribulations, as were not from the beginning of the creation which God created until now, neither shall be. And unless the Lord had shortened the days, no flesh should be saved: but for the sake of the elect which he hath chosen, he hath shortened the days. And then if any man shall say to you, Lo, here is Christ; lo, he is here: do not believe. For there will rise up false Christs and false prophets, and they shall shew signs and won-ders, to seduce (if it were possible) even the elect. Take you heed therefore; behold I have foretold you all things."

Before we ask ourselves what this text con-
tributes to our theme, we must first of all study it
very closely in order to determine what it actually
involves.

The language and images contained in this
paragraph are typically apocalyptic. The foremost
apocalyptic writer among the prophets of the Old
Testament was Daniel, and his book provides the
specific background for that part of the discourse
given by Jesus, particularly Daniel 11:21 ff.: the
visionary description of the persecution of God's
people in the Old Testament held under the rule of
the Syrian King Antiochus IV Epiphanes (175 till
164 B.C.). The apocalyptic language is principally
a symbolic language which likes to make use of
images to express ideas; therefore these images
should not be translated literally into historical and
profane realities. The significance of the symbolic
language becomes clear, however, by studying its
environment which is rooted in the Old Testament.

Jesus begins mysteriously with verse 14 by
saying: "And when you shall see the abomination
of desolation standing where it ought not (to be)."
This expression is taken from Daniel (compare 9:27;
12:11; and in St. Matthew's gospel it is recorded
specifically that this is the "abomination of desolation" of which Daniel spoke prophetically). In
the Old Testament the contemptuous expressions
"abomination" or "monster" are often used to describe a pagan idol. Daniel in spirit foresees that
such an "abomination" will be placed in the Temple
of Jerusalem, the place of God's presence on earth.

Now compare Daniel 11:31: "And arms shall stand
on his part, and they shall defile the sanctuary of
strength, and shall take away the continual sacri-
fice, and they shall place *there* the abomination
unto desolation." In Judaism the fulfillment of these
prophetic words was witnessed by the fact that in
the year 168 B.C. the above mentioned King Antiochus IV, the cruel persecutor of those who were
of the Jewish religion and with whom we are familiar from reading the books of the Machabees,
ordered an "abominable idol of desolation" to be
erected and venerated on the site of the sacrificial
altar in the Temple of Jerusalem where daily sacrifices, according to the law, were offered to God.
(compare I Mach. 1:54–59). Then Jesus says that
this terrible prediction of the prophet will find its
fulfillment only at the end of time. In order to be
able to understand exactly what Jesus was refer-
ring to, these events which occurred at the time of
the Machabees must be kept in mind constantly.
Jesus says of this "abomination of desolation" that
it will stand where it ought not to be; literally translated, He even says that *he* will stand where he
ought not to be, although the Greek expression for
"abomination" is neuter. In accordance with this
linguistic formulation and with the prophecies
made by Daniel and their temporary fulfillment
under Antiochus IV, it is clear that the expression
"abomination of desolation" was not used to describe the destruction of the Temple, because there
is not the least allusion made to that in our text. It
was intended rather that a personal being be char-

acterized, an individual, one that will force his way into the sanctuary and stand there like a divine statue to which are offered sacrifices. This reminds us naturally of another text in Holy Scripture, namely, of the second letter of the Apostle Paul to the Thessalonians, where he says the day of the Lord will not come "unless . . . there come a revolt first, and the man of sin be revealed, the son of perdition, who opposeth, and is lifted up above all that is called God, or that is worshipped, so that he sitteth in the temple of God, shewing himself as if he were God" (2:3-4). Here, according to tradition, the Apostle speaks of the Antichrist who "is to come" before Christ returns, and "whose coming is according to the working of Satan, in all power, and signs, and lying wonders, and in all seduction of iniquity to them that perish; because they receive not the love of the truth, that they might be saved" (2:9). This description of the Antichrist is influenced greatly by the book of Daniel. Similar expressions are used by the prophet to describe King Antiochus IV (compare Daniel 11:36): "And the king shall do according to his will, and he shall be lifted up, and shall magnify himself against every God. . . ." Presumably the Apostle takes his lead to describe the Antichrist and his works from a Jewish tradition which saw in Antiochus a prefiguration and a type of the coming Antichrist at the end of time.

No longer can there be any doubt that with His prophetic vision of the "abomination of desolation" Jesus meant the Antichrist who will "stand," as the apocalyptic language expresses so obscurely, in the sanctuary where "he ought not to be." The Antichrist penetrated the sanctuary of God, not to destroy it but to place himself there, instead of God, and to accept there divine homages from the whole world. It is unlikely that Jesus had in mind a specific place where the Antichrist will claim the rights of God, as for example the Temple of Jerusalem, for this temple will not be in existence at the time of the Antichrist. The location from which the Antichrist will operate remains a secret in that mysterious apocalyptic language. The most that can be mentioned about this point—since "Judea" is mentioned in verse 14—is that the pronouncements of Jesus concerning the sacrileges committed by the Antichrist were geographically attributed to the Temple of Jerusalem, because the expositions in the book of Daniel about the godless ways of King Antiochus IV were used especially by Jesus as the Old Testament background for His eschatological description. Jesus confined Himself to the imagery used during His time. His references to the great tribulations that were to come upon God's people in the age of the Antichrist were already realized in part during the time of the Apostles as a prophetic sign of the events that were to come in the year 70— that being the destruction of the Temple of Jerusalem. The corresponding section in St. Luke serves better to clarify and confirm this point, for in the gospel of St. Luke there is a definite allusion made to the events that would take place in the year 70 (see Luke 21:20–24). In reality, however, Jesus does not speak of those events but of the tribulations that the Antichrist will bring, not upon the Jewish nation at the end of time, but upon the community of Jesus. It should be noted that the text of St. Mark neither mentions a city nor anything about its destruction or about the destruction of the Temple. Instead, the passage in St. Mark 13:14–23 must be seen simply as a continuation of the preceding one describing the persecutions of the disciples of Jesus, the only difference being that Jesus now speaks of the incomparable intensification, the height of these "tribulations" which will come upon the Church at the time of the Antichrist.

This tribulation will commence with the appearance of the Antichrist, who by his presumptuousness, forcefulness and insolence will penetrate God's abode where "he ought not to be." This persecution will be so terrible that a speedy flight would be the only possible escape. "All household articles will have to be left behind, and there will hardly be time enough to get one's wraps. Those who are pregnant or who give suck will be least able to cope with the pressures and hardships of this flight. Should this flight have to take place during winter or at the time of the rains, the downpours, and the rivers which will be swollen way out of proportion, causing bottomless roads, will hinder this flight and make everything all the more difficult" (J. Schmid). This persecution, then, will fall upon the community of Jesus with a tremendous impact.

In verse 19, Jesus says that this "tribula-lation" will be so great that the likes of which have never been seen since the beginning of the world, nor will they ever be seen again. This implies that the expression "tribulation" cannot be attributed to the cosmic events which are expected to transpire in connection with the coming of Christ, for these events will only take place after "the tribulation" as St. Mark states explicitly in verses 13 and 24. The Greek expression for "tribulation" is generally used in the New Testament to describe the sufferings undergone during a persecution, sufferings which give testimony to the faith. The persecution of the Church through the Antichrist will be the most terrible of all times. If God did not shorten those days, for the sake of His elect, practically all men would become victims of this persecution. Its time will be shortened by the arrival of the Son of Man, by Christ's Parousia, and the way this will be manifested becomes clear in the interpretation of the text found in St. Mark's gospel (13:24–27). St. Paul formulates it quite similarly: "And then the wicked one shall be revealed whom the Lord Jesus shall kill with the spirit of his mouth; and shall destroy with the brightness of his coming . . ." (II Thess. 2:8; compare with Apoc. 19:11–21).

The terrible tribulations to which the Church will be subjected in the time of the Antichrist will consist, not only of the bloody persecutions of the select, but mainly of a most hazardous confusion among the faithful, caused by false announcements and rumors which will be spread everywhere: "Behold he is in the desert." Behold *he* is (hidden) in the inner chambers (Matt. 24:26). These claims and rumors will be capable of bewildering the minds of men. Men will thus fall prey to them as indeed many have already done today, though Jesus warned them explicitly. The Jehovah's Witnesses, for example, have declared that the coming of Christ has already taken place. The first time in October 1874, and then again in April 1878. Later on, they declared that October 1, 1914, would be the day, though they now say that Christ's return had been an invisible one (compare "*he* is in the inner chamber," i.e., in a hidden place!). Of course no such statement about the coming of Jesus can be confirmed in this way; consequently, everything is left to the imagination. The Apostle Paul had to refute that type of rumor; we have only to compare this with II Thessalonians (2:1–3), where it says: "And we beseech you brethren, by the coming of Our Lord Jesus Christ, and of our gathering together unto him: That you be not easily moved from your senses nor be terrified, neither by spirit, nor by word, nor by epistle, as sent from us, as if the day of the Lord were at hand. Let no man deceive you by any means. . . ." At the time of the Antichrist, confusing rumors like these will be spread more and more throughout the world. "Do not believe them," says Jesus, because everything will be quite different: "For as lightning cometh out of the east, and appeareth even into the west: so shall also the coming of the Son of man be" (Matt. 24:27; Luke 17:24; also Apoc. 3:3). Thus, the coming of Christ will be a sudden and unexpected one, visible to all men; it will not take place invisibly or in secrecy.

Besides these rumors concerning a secret return of the Son of Man which was supposed to have taken place already, false Christs and false prophets will arise in the time of the Antichrist according to St. Mark (13:22), and with various signs and miracles will try to seduce even the elect, estranging them from the true Christ. Probably the helpers of the Antichrist signify those persons who are bent on securing men for Satan by "signs and miracles" contained in modern techniques.

It is important for the Christian to know more about the New Testament's teaching regarding the Antichrist—and this importance becomes greater, the closer we come to the end of time. Only then will the Christian be able to recognize the true background of world history and assume that attitude of sobriety and watchfulness which is supposed to single him out according to the gospel.

The expression "Antichrist" belongs to the New Testament though it appears only in the first epistle of St. John (2:18): ". . . you have heard that Antichrist cometh . . . ," but St. John adds quickly that even now many Antichrists have (already) risen, and with this he refers to the appearance of heretics who attacked the traditional Christology of the Church (the teaching about Christ); see also (2:22): "Who is a liar, but he who denieth that Jesus is the Christ?" (the divine Messias). "This is Antichrist, who denieth the Father, and the Son." To this must be added: "And every spirit that dissolveth Jesus, is not of God: and this is Antichrist, of whom you have heard that he cometh and he is now al-

ready in the world" (4:3). The Greek text brings out
clearly that this last statement does not refer to the
Antichrist himself but rather to his spirit, to the sen-
timent of the Antichrist. The Apostle wishes to say
that the attack upon the apostolic doctrine of Christ
springs from the spirit of the Antichrist. The Antichrist will attempt to deprive Jesus Christ of the
dignity belonging to His divine kingship by denying
that Jesus is the Christ. It should also be noted that
John points to the coming of the Antichrist as to
something that the readers of his letter presumably
have "heard" of during the instructions held in the
community and in sermons given by the Apostles.
An example of these sermons about the figure and
work of the Antichrist was contained in the previ-
ously mentioned passage of St. Paul (II Thess. 2:3
ff.), though there the concept of "Antichrist" is not
used explicitly; further (in II Thess. 2:9), the appearance of the Antichrist is mentioned expressly
as a "Parousia" (an arrival) and is therefore con-
trasted to the Parousia of the Lord. Just as Christ
will appear to establish the kingdom of God once
and for all, so will the Antichrist appear before Him,
to try to establish the kingdom of Satan.

In the thirteenth chapter of the Apocalypse
of St. John the work of the Antichrist is described
with visions conveying tremendous force by using
the image of a terrible beast which rises from the
sea (13:1). This beast has received power from the
"dragon," that is, Satan (13:2–4; 20:2) and is adored
by men (13:4), "and he opened his mouth to dread-
ful blasphemies against God, to blaspheme his

name and his tabernacle and them that dwell in heaven" (13:6). The beast is at war with "the Lamb," that is, with Christ and His Saints and His community (13:6–7; 17:14; 19:19). "And power was given him over every tribe and people and nation" (13:7); "the kings of the earth serve him with their power" (17:12; 19:19). The Antichrist who is also characterized as a personal figure will thus represent the strongest political power in world-history! He will establish a godless kingdom in the world and he will dominate its entire economical force (see 13:17): "And that no man might buy or sell, but he hath the character or the name of the beast . . ."; also, "For thy merchants were the great men of the earth . . ." (18:23).

This first beast, which is a symbol of the Antichrist, is seen in the vision together with a second one which serves the first beast and propagates its principles in a priestly manner. ". . . and he caused the earth, and them that dwell therein, to adore the first beast . . ." (13:12). "And he did signs, so that he made also fire to come down from heaven unto the earth. . . . And he seduced them that dwell on the earth, for the signs which were given to him to do in the sight of the beast . . ." (13:13–14). This second beast makes an idol of the first one which all men adore "and should cause, that who-soever will not adore the image of the beast, should be slain" (13:15). The second beast, which is identical with the "false prophets" (compare 16:3; 19:20; 20:10), sees to it that the first beast, the Antichrist, is adored by all men and nations as a new

god instead of the true "King of ages," as God is
called (15:3). Thus, there is also a connection between the anti-Christian power held at the end of
time and the then-prevailing anti-Christian world-
view, a kind of state-religion, which everybody has
to confess if he does not want to become a martyr.
Therefore the Church at the end of time will be a
church of martyrs and all her previous glory will
have disappeared.

In conclusion, one might say that the Antichrist, or rather this anti-Christian power held at
the end of time, will be the strongest, politically and
economically, that has ever existed in this world.
The kingdom of the Antichrist will encompass the
whole world. It will also represent a spiritual power
which will proclaim a new faith to take the place of
the old one. But the Lamb will conquer the Antichrist and the world (17:4; 19:20–21).

"Take you heed therefore; behold I have
foretold you all things." With these words of Jesus
the passage (13:14–23) in St. Mark ends. Do not allow yourselves to be misled by these events if everything points to the contrary. The great temptation
to which the Church will be exposed at the time of
the Antichrist will not only be that of falling away
from the Faith in order to escape persecution, but
also that of believing in the weakness of God because of the seemingly helpless abandonment of the
Church to the Antichrist and his power. At this
time, then, much courage and faith, great patience
and a deep loyalty to the words of Holy Scripture
will be needed. The words of Holy Scripture can

help us maintain a serious view of things and enable us to distinguish between truth and heresy. But the pronouncements of Jesus about these terrible things at the end of time also contain a promise full of consolation. God will shorten these days of tribulation under the Antichrist; they will not last very long. God Himself will intervene and bring the furious assaults of the Antichrist against the community of the true Christ to a sudden end. As to how this will happen is the next subject to be treated in this text.

CHAPTER 6

*The Parousia (the Coming) of the Son of Man
(Mark 13:24–27)*

"But in those days, after that tribulation, the sun
shall be darkened, and the moon shall not give her
light (compare Isa. 13:10). And the stars of heaven
shall be falling down, and the powers that are in
heaven, shall be moved (compare Isa. 34:4). And
then shall they see the Son of man coming in the
clouds (compare Dan. 7:13), with great power and
glory. And then shall he send his angels, and shall
gather together his elect from the four winds (compare Zech. 2:6–10), from the uttermost part of the
earth to the uttermost part of heaven" (compare
Deut. 30:4).

The purpose of all teachings concerning the
Apocalypse, taken either from the Bible or from
other sources, is to explain to its readers the way
they are to visualize and understand the hard fate
awaiting them if they are persecuted. Because
these persecutions are the indispensable occurrences of an interim period, and because those who
have to endure these sufferings should not allow
themselves to be shaken and confused in their faith,
a special message is conveyed to them thereby, im-

plying: You are not abandoned! This is also what the synoptic apocalypse announces: Christ will show Himself to be the stronger; He will save you and precisely at a time when it will seem that everything is lost. That is why the coming of the Son of Man is primarily proclaimed as the day of the Church's deliverance. The text of St. Luke brings this out very clearly: "But when these things begin to pass, look up, and lift up your heads, because your redemption is at hand" (21:28). The whole synoptic apocalypse is concerned mainly with the followers of Jesus and as such the entire Church. Actually, it is the attitude of Christ's disciples in this interim period, their fate and their final salvation through the heavenly Son of Man, that is treated here. It was not intended to describe the various stages of world history; rather it was written as a book of consolation for the Church in a time of persecutions, the same as that composed by St. John. The Church should be informed about the final outcome and be able to recognize the signs which will precede the coming end. It is assumed that the teachings of Jesus about these eschatological events were gathered later to form one single volume during the persecution of the early Church under Nero, thus providing a book of consolation for the harassed Christians. Just as thirty years later, John gave the Church his Apocalypse when she was again badly persecuted under the emperor Domitian, whom many thought to be the Antichrist. Because the synoptic apocalypse was intended primarily as a book of consolation for the faithful, it does not contain a complete description of the so-called destruction of the world. The main question treated here is concerned, instead, with the way the Church will be saved from the terrible tribulations caused by the Antichrist. And the answer given by Jesus is: The Church will be saved by the arrival of the divine Son of Man.

This arrival will be preceded "after the days of tribulation" by a violent concussion of all cosmic forces, described with words taken from the Old Testament and according to the viewpoint held by the world of antiquity. This vision is most powerful and impresses us today as much as it did the contemporaries of Jesus. One should, however, pay closer attention to the text of the gospel, because these are the pronouncements which are often misunderstood by some readers and are, as a result, difficult to grasp. One should also consider that the Bible is not a textbook on natural science, and that the events described are written in a manner which is comprehensible and suitable for the man of that age. The images it depicts in our minds are certainly grandiose, but one should be careful not to intellectualize them one-sidedly. The fact that catastrophes of cosmic proportions are a possibility has been once more brought to our attention by what modern technique has developed recently. If, for example, the explosions of ten cobalt bombs suffice to destroy all life on this earth, then this would certainly represent a cosmic catastrophe of overwhelming consequence. ". . . the sun shall be darkened, and the moon shall not give her light. And the stars of heaven shall be falling down, and the powers that are in heaven shall be moved" (Mark 13: 24–25). Nearly all of these words which Jesus uses to describe those terrible events are taken from the Old Testament. The earth is not part of all this; everything takes place more or less in the upper regions. Men will react with fear, despair, and anxiety, St. Luke says (2:25–26). But at first nobody will understand what this means and there will be much consternation and dismay about these happenings. However, these collisions in the upper regions of space should not be regarded as an isolated factor but as one closely connected to the coming of the Son of Man. Actually, the powers of heaven will be moved because the Son of Man will leave His heavenly throne—believed to be situated at the uttermost point of heaven, according to biblical and ancient views—and He will penetrate all heavenly spaces with great power and glory, thus causing this very movement. The expression "great power" with which the Son of Man will come is a manifestation of the hosts of angels who will accompany Him and act as His courtiers, as verse 27 says so expressly. The concept "glory" (*doxa*) used in the Bible signifies "light" as well as "power" and serves mainly to describe the intrinsic atmosphere of God. According to the Bible, whenever God "appears" to a human being, man is left with the impression of light and power. Now we are able to understand why the light of the sun and the moon will fade away; it will fade away because a much stronger light will be manifested in heaven. It is the divine and brilliant form of the Son of Man in whose radiance the sun and the moon will cease to shine. The Son of Man together with His angels penetrates the heavenly spaces with such violence that the firmament where the stars are set, according to the old biblical view (compare Gen. 1:14–17), is shaken. The gospel's text does not tell us that the stars fall upon the earth; we do not know where they will "fall." But this whole description of future events is of no importance in itself; it does not signify "the destruction of the world" and therefore it cannot actually be called a "catastrophe." It is only meant to illustrate the tremendous power with which the Son of Man will come; the way this was threatened by God in the Old Testament through the prophet Aggai (2:6) to demonstrate His power over the whole universe. "For thus saith the Lord of hosts: Yet one little while and I will move the heaven and the earth and the sea and the dry land." Thus, the movement of the heavenly bodies is an act which belongs to the coming of Christ; it is the inauguration of His return: The Son of Man leaves the divine throne of heaven, penetrates all the spaces of heaven with the tremendous power of His angelic armies, causing them to be shaken, and then appears to men on the clouds of heaven, which serve God as His chariot, according to the belief held in the Old Testament. The Parousia is therefore an Epiphany, a manifestation of the heavenly world in whose center the radiant Son of Man appears shining with divine glory and surrounded by a host of angels.

Here the expression "Son of Man" with which we are familiar from the gospels must be explained briefly. This expression plays an important role in the book of the prophet Daniel. He sees in a vision one who looks like a son of man and who is brought before God, and God "gave him power and glory and a kingdom." It is through him that God holds the Last Judgment over the godless kingdoms of the world, represented in the prophet's vision by figures of beasts. The human figure in Daniel's vision, indicating the heavenly Son of Man, assumed, in Late Judaism, the traits of the Messianic "Servant of God," as mentioned by the prophet Isaias. Jesus chose the title "Son of Man" to characterize Himself and to ascertain His rights: I am He to whom God has given a heavenly kingdom and the power to judge the whole world (see John 5:27). At the time of the process before the High Council in Jerusalem, Jesus once more confirmed this solemnly when the high priest asked Him: "Art thou the Christ, the Son of the blessed God?" And Jesus answered: "I am. And you shall see the Son of man sitting on the right hand of the power of God, and coming with the clouds of heaven" (Mark 14:61–62).

This promise of Jesus will be fulfilled when He comes again, says our text; then He will be seen coming on the clouds of heaven with great power and glory. It does not say that He will descend upon earth to a certain place. Rather, He will appear on the clouds of heaven which will form His throne, widely visible to all, and from there He will send His hosts of angels all over the world to gather and summon His dispersed elect, who had fled from the wrath of the Antichrist. They will be gathered in a place which remains unmentioned. Christ, upon returning, will gather His community on earth and lead it triumphantly home to His heavenly kingdom, thereby saving the elect from the tribulations of the Antichrist. We are not told anything about the fate of the Antichrist in the synoptic apocalypse. One might read about this in the second letter to the Thessalonians and especially in the Apocalypse of St. John. St. Matthew goes beyond St. Mark in telling us about the Last Judgment which will be held by the Son of Man (see Matt. 25: 31–46).

Psalm 49 (1–5) in particular is used as a background for this whole section by St. Mark (13: 24–27): "The God of gods, the Lord hath spoken: and he hath called the earth. From the rising of the sun to its going down thereof. . . .God shall come manifestly: our God *shall come,* and shall not keep silence. A fire shall burn before him: and a mighty tempest *shall be* round about him. He shall call heaven from above, and the earth, to judge his people. Gather ye together his saints to him: who set his covenant before sacrifices." When the Son of Man comes back, these words of God will finally be fulfilled.

But when will this be? The answer to this will be given by adhering closely to the rest of the text in the synoptic apocalypse.

CHAPTER 7

The "When" of the End
(Mark 13:28–32)

"Now of the fig tree learn ye a parable. When the branch thereof is now tender, and the leaves are come forth, you know that summer is very near. So you also when you shall see these things come to pass, know ye that it is very nigh, even at the doors. Amen, I say to you, that this generation shall not pass, until all these things be done. Heaven and earth shall pass away, but my word shall not pass away. But of that day or hour no man knoweth, neither the angels in heaven, nor the Son, but the Father."

On Mount Olivet the Apostles asked Jesus about the "when" and the "sign" of the end of time. Now, at last, a definite answer is given to them, but it sounds negative because the hour, the exact "when," is known only to God! In interpreting this text it is better to begin with the last sentence of this paragraph and after that conclude with the parable of the fig tree.

At first, Jesus begins with an assertion: "Amen, I say to you, that this generation shall not pass, until all these things be done." "These things" can only be a reference to "all" the things which Jesus talked about in the preceding paragraph: to the wars, the famines, and persecutions of Christ's disciples and to the great tribulation under the Antichrist as well as the Parousia of the Son of Man. But which "generation" is it that will not pass until then? It has been said that Jesus thereby meant His contemporaries including the Apostles, but this would lead to the conclusion that Jesus had the same opinion of the early Church regarding the so-called expectancy of His return within the near future. Consequently, this sentence might imply: You can rely completely on what I have told you because you will experience all this during your own lifetime. On the other hand, this could mean that Jesus was entirely mistaken about such an important question, for since Jesus said all this, nearly two thousand years have passed, and the world still exists, and Christ has not as yet come back. Besides the fact that Jesus cannot possibly be in error, the explanation of this sentence is a very superficial one and does not express its true significance. Jesus predicted something far more profound and gave us a very decisive and important promise—a promise which involves an infallible sign to test the accuracy of His words, for us men of the twentieth century as well. How is this so and in which way?

The expression "this generation" may have a temporary significance in the sense of "contemporary," but it may also imply something pertaining to the kind and quality of the subject, as for example "this faithless, this adulterous generation" (compare Matt. 11:16; 12:29, 41, 42; 16:4; 17:17; Mark 8:12; Luke 11:29; and, further, Deut. 32:5; Ps. 94:10; Acts 2:40; Phil. 2:15). Coming from the lips of Jesus, this saying refers to the Jewish race and thus in our passage the expression "this generation" has a similar significance, namely, that it is the generation of the Jews which will experience "all this" in the course of time and that it will not die out before "all this happens." Though the Temple will be destroyed, as Jesus had foretold at the beginning of the paragraph, and though the Jewish people will be dispersed into all four corners of the world up to our present days (see Luke 21:24) and though "this generation" will be deprived of its natural habitat, it will not pass till all this happens, not until the Son of Man will come back on the clouds of heaven. The simply inexplicable historical continuance of the Jewish people in spite of the great catastrophe of the year 70, and the continued existence of "this generation" through all ages until the Last Day is a sure sign— Jesus wishes to say—that all this will happen and that His words will be fulfilled. The existence of the Jewish people throughout the ages of history is the great sign for all other nations that the words of God and of Jesus are truthful, that they are truth itself. For the existence of this people lasting in spite of its dispersion through two thousand years among all the other nations on earth, which seems to be drawing to an end only in our present day, is simply inexplicable from the natural point of view. It is a constant miracle of history

which can only be explained on the grounds that it
is God who leads these people in a special way.

At the same time, these words of Jesus are
also a promise that the Jewish people will not perish until the Messias returns. For they also—that
"generation"—will receive Christ when He comes
back and will also cry out: "Blessed is he that cometh in the name of the Lord" (see Matt. 23:29; Luke
13:35; see also Rom. 11:25, where St. Paul speaks
about this "mystery" in saying that "blindness in
part has happened in Israel, until the fullness of the
Gentiles should come in").

Thus it is this perpetual existence of the Jewish people, leading to the Lord's Parousia, that the
Christian should take as a sure sign of the reliability of what Jesus had promised; for the continual
existence of the Jewish people all through the course
of history, in spite of the hard fate imposed upon
this people, is possible only because it is the will of
God. And that is why the Christian should always
respect the children of Israel.

Jesus, then, confirms all this with an added
assertion: "Heaven and earth shall pass away, but
my word shall not pass away." The phrase "heav-
en and earth" is an expression used in the Bible to
indicate the whole universe, all of creation. Thus
the certainty and absoluteness of Jesus' words is
far greater than the apparently unshakable continuance of the universe. The statement "heaven and
earth shall pass away" must therefore be understood in a conditional sense, that is, in the sense of
a supposition: Even if heaven and earth should

pass, rest assured, My words will not pass; they will be fulfilled!

Thus Jesus strongly emphasizes the certainty and reliability of His words about all these things. But when will all this happen? When will the exact hour be, especially that of the Parousia? The Apostles wanted to know this and so do we. Jesus answers this question by saying: This is only known to the Father! Jesus does not answer this question the way men would like Him to. With this negative response Jesus refuted all further speculations, so characteristic for Late Judaism, concerning the "end." It is not possible to foresee the end the way the Jehovah's Witnesses and all other sectarians of our days try to do this, because the hour is known to the Father alone. (It says expressly "alone" in the gospel of St. Matthew.) Not even the angels in heaven nor the Son know this, Jesus adds. There was obviously much objection to this latter statement from the very start, as even St. Luke eliminated this verse from his gospel. Many who bore testimony to this text, a little later on, eliminated the part "but the Father alone" from the gospel of St. Matthew, 24:36. But it is precisely this objection that confirms the authenticity of these words of Jesus. "As a formulation created by the archcommunity, this sentence is unthinkable" says J. Schmid. However, at this point Jesus speaks as a man and not as God. The hour of "that day"—and this biblical expression means God's Day—which will inaugurate the Last Judgment of this world is unknown entirely. Therefore it is senseless to make calculations, and it is nothing more than human presumption in the face of God's word to declare that we will see this day in our present age, the way this has been stated by the aged archapostle of Frankfort, the leader of the "New Apostles," who proclaim that the Lord will appear during his lifetime. God was supposed to have revealed this to him in 1951. If not even the Son knows this hour, nor the angels in heaven, then God will certainly not reveal it to the leader of a sect. These are human presumptions which the true Christian who is obedient to the words of God should be careful to avoid. Nobody knows the hour—this is the answer Jesus gives to His Apostles after they ask Him about the "when." But what about the other question, concerning the "sign" or presign which might serve as an indication for the approaching end? To answer this we must now consider the parable of the fig tree.

In order to better understand what this parable is supposed to express in the synoptic apocalypse, the best approach would be to ask first what the text really contains and what it does not contain. It does not say: when the fig tree brings forth leaves then summer is near; but rather: when the fig tree brings forth leaves this is a sign for all that summer is near, for only then can one be sure that summer is coming. The "story" of this parable is particularly understandable for the Oriental. All through the winter the fig tree looks dried out and dead, but in spring, within a very short time, it grows large branches covered with juicy leaves—and this is the infallible sign for everybody that summer is close at hand. Now summer will not tarry any longer; it is approaching rapidly, for the green, juicy twigs of the fig tree announce its coming with certainty. Thus it is not the nearness of summer but the sure sign of its approach that this parable is mainly concerned about.

And so it is also concerning My return, is what Jesus wants to say. Then there is also something by which it will be "known" that its coming is at hand, namely, "when these things come to pass." To what can this refer? It cannot refer to the movements in the spaces of heaven, because these are only accompanying symptoms of the Parousia itself which is already taking place when they occur. It can only refer to the immediately preceding tribulations of the Church, during the time of the Antichrist. It is this great tribulation, existing the way "it never was nor shall be" which Christians should and must recognize as a "sign" that the coming of the Lord, and consequently also that the "end," is at hand. This is important for the Christian to know, for some might lose their courage during these terrible persecutions of the Antichrist. The Christian might then be tempted to think and speak similarly to those who mock and doubt, according to the second letter of St. Peter (3:4): "Where is his promise or his coming?" for Jesus is not coming to save us, after all! The Lord retaliates by saying: It is precisely this circumstance, the fact that you see "this" happening, namely, the terrible persecution of My Church by the Antichrist, which will be the infallible sign to be recognized and "known" by you, that my coming and the end are at hand. Thus, according to Jesus, the faithful will receive a visible "sign" for the approaching end of the world. It is the appearance of the Antichrist and his violent assault on the community of Jesus. Within history, the Parousia of the Antichrist leads to the termination of the world.

And when will the Antichrist appear? Jesus does not respond to that question, and therefore it is useless to try to give an exact answer. But as we stated before, and according to Holy Scripture, the Antichrist will be represented by the strongest political and economic power in world-history. He will be a very realistic figure of history and belongs, according to Revelation, to the concrete history of mankind. In St. John (I–2:18) it says that there are "already now" many antichrists at work. They are those heretics and seducers who deny the existence of God and His Son, and the divine dignity of Christ. Thus the Antichrist has his precursors and his works, his "face," will be made visible in a typical fashion by his followers who act, so to speak, as models for the Antichrist and who will appear toward the end of time. Inasmuch as Christ has His precursors in the prophets of the Old Testament, the Antichrist also has his precursors, and their works and attitude will betray and make evident for us, more or less clearly, the intentions and plans of the Antichrist.

Though we are in no position to answer the question about the time of the Antichrist's arrival, we may, on the other hand, give serious thought to the following question and even try to answer it. Is history and the present condition of the world gradually ripening for the world-wide activities of the Antichrist, the way it is described in Holy Scripture? Has history progressed to the point that the appearance of the Antichrist is a possibility? There is probably also a "fullness of time" for him just as there was one for the appearance of Jesus in this world (see Mark 1:15; Gal. 4:4; Eph. 1:10). In answer to this question, a few points which are noteworthy should be stressed. For Ignaz Doellinger, the renowned Church historian of Munich, who in 1870 refuted the dogma of the Pope's infallibility, it was "quite unthinkable," that some day there should exist a world power which "would close all churches in all parts of the world and on all islands, simultaneously." At the time, Doellinger was obviously incapable of imagining that the world might be ruled some day from one single seat, the way Holy Scripture presupposes this for the working of the Antichrist. Today, after only eighty years, this is no longer a problem. Now it is possible to govern the world from one place; technically the world is ripe for just that. We have anti-Christian worldviews, as for example dialectic materialism, and these views do not only preoccupy the minds of a few philosophers and politicians, but they have already far-reaching effects and claim to be a universally approved doctrine of salvation. So there is good reason to believe and state that the condition of our present age could certainly set the stage for the appearance and work of the Antichrist, as described by Holy Scripture. History is ripe for that time. Modern sociology already speaks of "the feasibility of history's termination." But we do not know whether the Antichrist will really appear in the near future, and we should be careful about this kind of prediction and be truly mindful of the warnings of Jesus with regard to seducers and false prophets. However, there is no doubt that history and the world are fully ripe for the appearance of the Antichrist, and in any event this awareness calls for intense watchfulness and earnestness on the part of the Christian, even if we do not know the "hour."

CHAPTER 8

Jesus Admonishes Us to be Watchful
(Mark 13:33–37)

"Take ye heed, watch and pray. For ye know not
when the time is. Even as a man who going into a
far country, left his house; and gave authority to
his servants over every work, and commanded the
porter to watch. Watch ye therefore (for you know
not when the lord of the house cometh: at even, or
at midnight, or at the cockcrowing, or in the morn-
ing): Lest coming on a sudden, he find you sleeping. And what I say to you, I say to all: Watch."

At the end of His teaching Jesus urges us to
be especially watchful as the hour of the Parousia
is quite uncertain. For this purpose He chooses, according to the gospel of St. Mark, the form of a
short parable. The story goes thus: A man—in
verse 35 he is called the lord of the house—goes on
a journey, and during the time of his absence he
leaves all authority for the administration of his
property to his servants. It is the same authority
which he himself possesses, and in addition he as-
signs a special task to each one of his servants. The
doorkeeper who receives the keys of the house is
particularly admonished to be watchful, so as to be

able to open the gate immediately in case his master should return suddenly during the night.

This story conceals a religious and historical reality of salvation, for Jesus Himself is hidden behind the "lord of the house." He is the "man" who, in a way, goes on a "journey" at His Ascension and leaves the care of His "house," that is, of His Church—in the New Testament the Church is called the "house of God"—to His "servants," the Apostles, conferring upon them the same "authority" which the Lord Himself possesses. All of them have received a task. The "doorkeeper" has been entrusted with a special one, that is, to remain watchful and wait for the return of the Lord—apparently the doorkeeper was meant to be Peter, the Prince of the Apostles. The incalculable and therefore sudden return of the lord of the house signifies Christ's Parousia, His coming, and as its time is completely unknown, this calls for the constant readiness of the servants and especially that of the doorkeeper.

What Jesus demands of His disciples at first in the disguise of a parable is once again given as an open command: "Watch ye therefore, for you know not when the lord of the house cometh." At first the Apostles had asked Jesus about the "when"; now Jesus again answers by saying: You do not know when the Lord cometh. He may come soon but He may also tarry for a long time. Woe to you if He finds you sleeping as the rest of the world, or as the five foolish virgins who did not realize the bridegroom would come so soon and therefore thought they could go on sleeping since there would be enough time left to buy the oil for the lamps before receiving the bridegroom (see Matt. 25:1–13).

The eschatological events will come as a complete surprise for the whole world. It will be as in the days of Noah, according to St. Matthew (24:38–41): "For as in the days before the flood, they were eating and drinking, marrying and giving in marriage, even till that day in which Noe entered into the ark. And they knew not till the flood came, and took them all away; so also shall the coming of the Son of man be. Then two shall be in the field: one shall be taken, and one shall be left. Two women shall be grinding at the mill: one shall be taken, and one shall be left." This may also be compared to St. Paul (I Thess. 5:2–3): "For yourselves know perfectly, that the day of the Lord shall so come, as a thief in the night. For when they shall say, peace and security; then shall sudden destruction come upon them, as the pains upon her who is with child and they shall not escape." Thus, for the world, that day will come unexpectedly, as a complete surprise. Men will go about their business and pursue their pleasures just as on any other day; exactly as in the days of Noah. And God's judgment will come upon them wherever they might happen to be. One will be taken away into the kingdom of the Son of Man, the other one will be left outside to perish. We find very similar verses in the gospel of St. Luke (see 17:26–27, 34–35), but St. Luke adds these two (36–37): "They (the disciples) answering, say to him: Where, Lord? Who said to them: Wheresoever the body shall be, thither will the eagles also be gathered together." Where will the world be taken by surprise at the Parousia and the Last Judgment? According to the viewpoints of Late Judaism, the disciples obviously had a definite place in mind where these events will take place. But the answer of Jesus tells us that all this will not happen at a particular place in the world but wherever the "body" happens to be, that is, wherever there are human beings. The Parousia will not take place just anywhere in the world but everywhere at the same time. "Wherever there are men the judgment will take place; it will be thrust upon them" (J. Schmid) as eagles on a body.

In St. Mark's gospel the apocalyptic teaching of Jesus ends with the pronouncement: "And what I say to you, I say to all: Watch." We, who have delved into Holy Scripture to learn what Jesus teaches about eschatology, belong to "all these" as well. We did not inquire as to what Jesus said about the end of the world but, rather, what He teaches about the end of the world. For us Jesus Christ is not merely one among many others who give serious thought to the end of the world. For us Christians who are believers Jesus is *the* Teacher who pronounces the words of God. His words will not pass even if heaven and earth should pass. For us His word is the truth and gives us reliable information as to the question concerning the end of the world.

This "end of the world" does not belong, as already emphasized in the preface of this interpretation based on St. Mark's thirteenth chapter, to the order of nature but to that of history. Nature will participate in these eschatological events, just as nature was also part of what happened in a night of bombing during the last war; but the laws of growth and development in history differ from those of nature. Seen from the viewpoint of the order of nature and her laws, the world could go on existing for milliards of year; from the viewpoint of the order of history, it could end tomorrow. No one who views history seriously and attentively will be able to deny the predictions made by Jesus and say that these predictions have nothing to do with the true and concrete history of mankind. Modern man's consciousness of human history is definitely apocalyptic, and he knows that his existence, as well as that of the whole world, is basically menaced. Fear of the things that are to come clutches the hearts of all men, and even modern philosophy says that this fear belongs to the fundamental state of mind of modern man. Thus, what we experience historically today bears out that the word of Jesus must be recognized as a definite possibility within history. Today, no one is able to say, in all earnestness, that nothing will happen the way it was foretold by Jesus of Nazareth; rather, everybody will have to admit that there not only exist definite possibilities of things happening that way, but that much of what is going on leads to that conclusion, even if we do not know when and how soon this will take place.

However, in spite of all this, the Christian's heart should be free from all anxiety. "So you also when you shall see these things come to pass," then lift up your heads (full of hope and confidence) because your salvation is at hand. The Son of man will come to judge this world but He also will come to lead His own to their home in the eternal kingdom of His Father. Then God will finally be justified in the eyes of all, and that God may be justified in the face of the whole world is precisely the secret wish of every Christian.

One of the few words which the New Testament handed down to us in the native tongue of Jesus, in Aramaic, are: *Marana tha!* In English: Come, Lord Jesus! (see I Cor. 16:22). This is the way the early Church, at the time of the Apostles, called out to Him when the liturgy was celebrated. Is it not sad that, later on, Christians could scarcely summon the courage to repeat this call? But it seems that the time is gradually nearing, when we, with great and inmost longing in our hearts, will also call out once more in our prayers,

Come, Lord Jesus!

BIBLIOGRAPHY

K. Algermissen, *Christian Denominations* (St. Louis, Herder, 1946).

W. Bartz, *Falsche Propheten*, 5th Edition (Trier, 1956).

J. Danielou, *The Lord of History: Reflections on the Inner Meaning of History* (Chicago, H. Regnery, 1958).

Ph. Dessauer, "Die Politik des Antichrist," in *Wort und Wahrheit*, 6 (1951), 405–415.

Th. Haecker, *Der Christ und die Geschichte*, 2nd Edition (Munich, 1949).

K. Hutten, *Seher, Gruebler, Enthusiasten*, 4th Edition (Stuttgart, 1954).

J. H. Newman, *Der Antichrist nach der Lehre der Vaeter* (Munich, 1951).

E. Peterson, "Zeuge der Wahrheit," in *Theologische Traktate* (Munich, 1951).

J. Pieper, *The End of Time* (New York, Pantheon Books, 1954). Quotation from I. Doellinger taken from this book.

P. Riessler, *Altjuedisches Schrifttum ausserhalb der Bibel* (Augsburg, 1928).

H. Schlier, "Vom Antichrist," in *Die Zeit in der Kirche* (Freiburg, 1956).

J. Schmid, *Das Evangelium nach Matthaeus, Markus, Lukas* (Regensburger Neues Testament, Bd. 1–3), 3rd Edition (Regensburg, 1956).